124

High-Impact Letters for Busy Principals

124

High-Impact Letters for Busy Principals

A Guide to Handling Difficult Correspondence

Marilyn L. Grady

CORWIN PRESS, INC.
A Sage Publications Company
Thousand Oaks, California

For information:

Corwin Press, Inc.
A Sage Publications Company
2455 Teller Road
Thousand Oaks, California 91320
E-mail: order@corwinpress.com

Sage Publications Ltd.
6 Bonhill Street
London EC2A 4PU
United Kingdom

Sage Publications India Pvt. Ltd.
M-32 Market
Greater Kailash I
New Delhi 110 048 India

Printed in the United States of America

Library of Congress Cataloging-in-Publication Data

Grady, Marilyn L.
  124 high-impact letters for busy principals / by Marilyn L. Grady.
     p. cm.
  ISBN 0-7619-7663-9 (cloth: alk. paper)
  ISBN 0-7619-7664-7 (pbk.: alk. paper)
  1. School principals--Correspondence--Handbooks, manuals, etc. 2.
Form letters--Handbooks, manuals, etc. I. Title: One hundred
twenty-four high-impact letters for busy principals. II. Title.
  LB2831.9 .G72 2000
  651.7'52--dc21   00-008357

This book is printed on acid-free paper.

04   05   10   9   8   7   6   5   4   3

Corwin Editorial Assistant: Kylee Liegl
Production Editor: Nevair Kabakian
Editorial Assistant: Candice Crosetti
Typesetter/Designer: Danielle Dillahunt

Contents

Acknowledgments

To Kristy Carlson, Peggy Croy, and Harriet Gould, I owe a special note of thanks because they not only opened their letter files for me but also took the time to carefully and critically review the letters included in this collection. Thanks, too, to Patrick Hunter-Pirtle and Barb Marchese for sharing their letter collections. Phyllis Hasse lent her expertise to the preparation of this volume of letters. Her efforts are always outstanding and appreciated. For their patience and consistent good humor, I thank Alex, Natasha, Justin, and Elizabeth Grady.

About the Author

Marilyn L. Grady, PhD, is a professor of educational administration at the University of Nebraska-Lincoln. Her research areas include leadership, principalship, and superintendent-board relations. She has written for a number of journals, including *Planning and Changing, The High School Journal,* the *Journal of School Leadership,* and *Research in Rural Education.* She has more than 100 publications to her credit. Her editorial board service includes *Educational Administration Quarterly,* the *Rural Educator,* the *Journal of At-Risk Issues,* the *Journal of School Leadership, Advancing Women in Leadership On-Line Journal,* and the *Journal for a Just and Caring Education.*

She coordinates an annual conference on women in educational leadership that attracts national attendance and is in its 14th year. She has served on the executive boards of the National Council of Professors of Educational Administration, the Center for the Study of Small/Rural Schools, and Phi Delta Kappa Chapter 15. She is a member of the American Educational Research Association, the Horace Mann League, the International Academy of Educational Leaders, the Schoolmasters Club, the American Association of School Administrators, the National Rural Education Association, National Council of Professors of Educational Administration, the Midwest Educational Research Association, the International Academy of Educational Leaders, and Phi Delta Kappa.

She has been an administrator in kindergarten through 12th grade schools as well as at the college and university level. She received her BA in history from Saint Mary's College, Notre Dame, Indiana, and her PhD in educational administration with a specialty in leadership from Ohio State University.

Introduction

$\mathbf{M}$ary Poppins's direction that "well begun is half done" was the spirit guiding the preparation of this collection. The letters presented here and on the accompanying CD-ROM are intended as templates. They are meant to be a beginning. The templates have been designed to be generic, allowing the letter writers to personalize them to specific situations. Specialized language and educational jargon have been avoided so that the letters can be compatible with many different school settings.

The letters that can make a difference in the principalship are often the letters that principals have no time to prepare. Often, "must write" negative letters consume the principal's letter-writing energies. This collection of letters is primarily focused on the letters that principals have little or no time to prepare. Clearly, principals know how to write letters; they simply have incredible time constraints. The letters in this manual are not substitutes for the personalized letters that principals will craft. This collection is merely a starter kit.

The sequence of letters begins with the positives: thank-you letters, congratulations, best wishes, and other personal correspondence. These are the letters that build a culture of care throughout a school community. Recognition for a job well done or for a special contribution to the education of students are letters that make the work life of a school a positive experience. Remember: You can *never* write too many thank-you letters.

Letters that are short, simple, and sincere can convey the right touch to the recipient. Letters that are personal, such as condolence notes, should be handwritten.

The letters presented here are derived from a number of sources. Practicing principals contributed letters; these principals are cited in the acknowledgments. Other letters come from my files, from personal experiences as an administrator and teacher in elementary, junior high, and senior high settings. Letters have also been collected during years of association with principals, with schools, and from parenting five children.

Some letters get written because they simply must be written. These may fall under a heading of discipline or problem behaviors, and they often have legal implications. School attorneys often assist in the preparation of these formal letters. This collection of letters is not designed to address these sensitive issues. Often, state statutes and specific school district policies frame these letters, and template letters would not be appropriate.

Principals provide many types of correspondence. Teacher appraisals, special education reports, forms pertaining to various uses, and newsletters are other types of written communication. This collection does not include these. School districts have teacher appraisal procedures and accompanying documentation based on district policies. For individuals who do not work in districts with established procedures, *The Marginal Teacher*[1] is an excellent resource. Special education procedures and correspondence deserve a special collection of letters targeted to the participants in this process. There are a number of companies that provide education forms for schools. School newsletters are an important communication device. Newsletter samples would fill an entire notebook, too. For these reasons, these forms of correspondence are not included in this collection.

NOTE   1. *The Marginal Teacher: A Step-by-Step Guide to Fair Procedures for Identification and Dismissal*, by C. E. Lawrence, M. K. Vachon, D. O. Leake, and B. H. Leake, was published in 1993 in Newbury Park, CA, by Corwin Press (805/499-0721, Ext. 8234).

1

Thank-You Letters

Opportunities to say "thank you" abound. Yet the letters or notes do not get written. A principal who establishes a professional goal of crafting one thank-you note or letter per day will make great progress in establishing a positive climate for the principalship.

You can never write too many thank-you letters. Although the letters do not need to be long, they should be prompt, sincere, and personal. The occasions for thank-you letters or notes are seemingly endless:

Staff members who provide guidance to new teachers as mentors, who participate on interview teams, who assist students, or who serve on committees deserve a special note of thanks.

Students, too, must be thanked for their special help.

Parents need to be thanked for accompanying field trips, assisting with fundraisers, and serving on Parent-Teacher Associations.

Special guests of the school must be thanked for their contributions to the school program.

Speakers who make presentations may also be thanked for their positive influence on educational thinking.

Donors must certainly be thanked for their contributions.

Thank-You Letter 1.1
STAFF MENTOR

Elementary or Secondary

(Date)

(Name)

(Address)

Dear (Name):

Thank you for serving as a mentor to (Name) this year. Sharing your ideas and expertise about teaching has made this a rewarding and successful experience for (Name). Your investment in the mentoring process affects the teaching profession as a whole as well as student learning.

Thank you for your contributions to the mentoring program.

Sincerely,

Principal

Thank-You Letter 1.2
STAFF TEAM MEMBER

Elementary or Secondary

(Date)

(Name)

(Address)

Dear (Name):

Thank you for your willingness to serve on the Teacher Interview Team. I really enjoyed the opportunity to work with you in the process of hiring new staff members. The task is critical, but with many hands, the work involved in screening applications, conducting phone interviews, and identifying the top candidates was a success. The new process we've used during our past two screenings has really assisted us in identifying those who best match the philosophy of (Name of School) School.

I hope that you found the process enjoyable. As always, change and revision help to improve our work. Please take a few minutes to reflect on the process and provide me with any ideas you might have for improving it.

Again, *thank you* for your contributions.

Sincerely,

Principal

Thank-You Letter 1.3
STAFF MEMBER LEAVING SCHOOL

Elementary or Secondary

(Date)

(Name)

(Address)

Dear (Name):

Thank you for your service to (Name of School) School. During your tenure here, you worked hard toward making (Name of School) School's mission come true. Your ability to work with students is exceptional. The "extras" you provided to assist student learning helped the entire team. We will all miss your humor too.

I wish you the best in your new job. You will be missed by all of us.

Sincerely,

Principal

Thank-You Letter 1.4
STAFF COMMITTEE MEMBER

Elementary or Secondary

(Date)

(Name)

(Address)

Dear (Name):

Thank you for agreeing to serve on the (Name of Committee) Committee. This is an important assignment, and your work on the committee will affect the entire school district.

We look forward to hearing about the work of the committee.

Sincerely,

Principal

Thank-You Letter 1.5
STUDENT

Elementary or Secondary

(Date)

(Name)

(Address)

Dear (Student Name):

Thank you for your help with the (Activity) at (Name of School) School last week. You did a great job of organizing (Activity) and working with the younger students.

On behalf of everyone who participated in (Activity), thanks!

Sincerely,

Principal

Thank-You Letter 1.6
PARENT(S), FIELD TRIP

Elementary

(Date)

(Name)

(Address)

Dear (Name):

Thank you for accompanying the (Class) class on their field trip to (Place). The students have made many comments about what a fantastic time they had. They particularly appreciated your great sense of humor.

Field trips are a wonderful educational experience for students. Without your help, this student trip would not have been possible.

So on behalf of the students, thanks so much.

Sincerely,

Principal

Thank-You Letter 1.7
PARENT(S), FUNDRAISING

Elementary

(Date)

(Name)

(Address)

Dear (Name):

Thank you for your assistance with our recent (Event) fundraising event. Your efforts resulted in profits of (Dollar Amount) for (Name of School).

Successful fundraising activities take time and organization. The success of the (Event) is clear evidence of your outstanding work.

As you know, the students at (Name of School) realize the benefits of the fundraising activities. On their behalf, thank you for your work.

Sincerely,

Principal

Thank-You Letter 1.8
PARENT(S), PTO/PTA

Elementary

(Date)

(Name)

(Address)

Dear (Name):

Thank you for your service as PTO/PTA (Position) during the (Year) school year. This work is very important to the experiences our children have at (Name of School) School.

Your work this year has resulted in some real successes. These include (Description).

The true beneficiaries of your efforts are the students at (Name of School) School.

Again, thank you for your efforts.

Sincerely,

Principal

Thank-You Letter 1.9
GUEST SPEAKER(S) (1)

Elementary

(Date)

(Name)

(Address)

Dear (Name):

Thank you for giving your valuable time and sharing an important message with our students. It was an excellent presentation.

I also appreciate the involvement of (Names) and their important messages to the students. Their participation provided great role models for the students. Please extend our thanks to (Names).

There were many positive comments about the quality of your presentations.

Thanks for helping make (Description) Week a success.

Sincerely,

Principal

Thank-You Letter 1.10
GUEST SPEAKER (2)

Elementary or Secondary

(Date)

(Name)

(Address)

Dear (Name):

Thank you for the program you provided for our students. I am sure they will remember the experience. Your contributions are greatly appreciated!

Sincerely,

Principal

Thank-You Letter 1.11
CONFERENCE SPEAKER

Elementary or Secondary

(Date)

(Name)

(Address)

Dear (Name):

I really enjoyed your presentation at the (Name of Conference) Conference. I was particularly interested in what you said about (Description). I am sorry that all of our teachers were not able to attend the presentation.

Thank you for sharing your work in this area. It is really of critical importance to educators.

Sincerely,

Principal

Thank-You Letter 1.12
DONATION, GENERAL

Elementary or Secondary

(Date)

(Name)

(Address)

Dear (Name):

On behalf of the students at (Name of School) School, thank you for your generous contribution. The students at (Name of School) School will benefit from your contribution both now and in the future. In times of limited resources, contributions such as yours make an incredible difference in what's available to our students.

Your gift will truly be remembered at (Name of School) School.

Sincerely,

Principal

Thank-You Letter 1.13
DONATION, IN KIND

Elementary or Secondary

(Date)

(Name)

(Address)

Dear (Name):

On behalf of the students of (Name of School) School, I want to thank you for the donation of (Description) to our (Description) program.

Thank you for the support that (Name of Business) has shown (Name of School) School. We value your assistance and association with our school.

Sincerely,

Principal

Thank-You Letter 1.14
DONATION, MONEY

Elementary or Secondary

(Date)

(Name)

(Address)

Dear (Name):

Please accept this as a receipt for your generous donation to the (Description). Your donation to the (Name of School) during (Year) totaled (Dollar Amount).

Thank you for your generous support.

Sincerely,

Principal

2

Appreciation Letters

Like thank you letters, letters of appreciation should be written often. Many individuals deserve notes of appreciation as recognition for their efforts and the work they accomplish. Sometimes, we overlook opportunities to note these accomplishments because the work is "expected." However, principals can build a positive culture by acknowledging the "positives" in a school environment. Shifting the emphasis to what works and what's best in a school can build positive regard for all members of the school community. Individuals might receive appreciation letters for the following activities:

> *Staff members* working with students during a special appreciation week or driving a bus deserve special notes of appreciation.
>
> *Volunteers* who contribute their time and talent to a school deserve recognition and appreciation for their efforts.
>
> *Business partners* provide opportunities for students and needed resources for schools. There are many opportunities to recognize the roles business partners play for students and schools through letters of appreciation.

Appreciation Letter 2.1
STAFF, GENERAL

Elementary or Secondary

(Date)

(Name)

(Address)

Dear (Name):

Thank you for working with (Name). We really appreciate your efforts in (Description). You are truly an asset to our school.

Sincerely,

Principal

Appreciation Letter 2.2
STAFF, APPRECIATION WEEK

Elementary or Secondary

(Date)

(Name)

(Address)

Dear (Name):

Since this is a special week, I would like to take the opportunity to thank you for your fine work throughout the year.

Your work on behalf of our students really makes a difference. Thanks for your dedication and efforts.

Sincerely,

Principal

Appreciation Letter 2.3
STAFF, ROLE

Elementary or Secondary

(Date)

(Name)

(Address)

Dear (Name):

Thank you for your contributions to our staff and students in your role as a (Position). Your responsiveness to the many situations that have occurred at school has been exceptional. The staff and I appreciate your hard work and dedication.

The week of (Date) is set aside as (Position) Appreciation Week. On (Day of Week), a special breakfast will be held to honor (Position). On (Day of the Week) from (Time) to (Time), the staff will host a special luncheon for (Position) in the cafeteria.

We look forward to sharing this special week with you.

Sincerely,

Principal

Appreciation Letter 2.4
STAFF DRIVER

Elementary

(Date)

(Name)

(Address)

Dear (Name):

Thank you for being an important part of (Name of School) School. We certainly recognize that driving a school bus is not an easy job. Keeping students seated and quiet while driving safely is serious work.

To recognize your contributions, we have set aside (Date) as Bus Driver Appreciation Day. On that day, from (Time) to (Time) a.m., we will have coffee and refreshments for our bus drivers in the school cafeteria. We look forward to sharing this special day with you.

Sincerely,

Principal

Appreciation Letter 2.5
VOLUNTEER

Elementary or Secondary

(Date)

(Name)

(Address)

Dear (Name):

Thank you for your many contributions to (Name of School). Please accept the enclosed Certificate of Appreciation for volunteering in the (Description). The students and teachers have certainly appreciated your assistance.

We hope you will continue to be involved with school activities!

Sincerely,

Principal
Enclosure

Appreciation Letter 2.6
BUSINESS PARTNER

Elementary or Secondary

(Date)

(Name)

(Company Name)

(Address)

Dear (Name):

(Name of School) School is fortunate to have (Name of Business) as our school's business partner. We appreciate the many ways you have assisted the students and the school. Your presence in the classrooms and the mentoring of students has been particularly helpful.

Visiting your workplace was a memorable experience for the students. Not only did the students enjoy seeing (Business) but they returned to school more excited about the "world of work."

We are very fortunate to have (Name of Business) as our business partner. I hope this partnership will last for many years.

Sincerely,

Principal

Appreciation Letter 2.7
BUSINESS PARTNER, INVITATION

Elementary

(Date)

(Name)

(Company Name)

(Address)

Dear (Name):

On (Day of the Week), (Date), the (Students) of (Name of School) are sponsoring a (Event) in the cafeteria from (Time) to (Time). This (Event) will benefit the clubs and activities at (Name of School) School.

In appreciation for all that (Name of Business) does for (Name of School), we are enclosing two complimentary tickets for you and a guest to join us at the (Event). We hope to see you soon!

Sincerely,

Principal

3

Congratulations Letters

Many life events, as well as personal and professional accomplishments, deserve a personal note of congratulations. Often, these events slip by unnoticed or unheralded by principals. These events provide excellent opportunities for principals to extend recognition to those associated with the school. Building good will and a culture of accomplishment should be important goals for a principal.

> *Teachers* might be congratulated for exhibitions of student work, receiving awards, being elected to office, completing advanced degrees, the birth of a child, promotions, or student performance.
>
> *Parents* might be congratulated for their child's receipt of an award, accomplishments, recognition in the newspaper, receipt of a scholarship, or winning a contest.
>
> *Students* might be recognized for winning awards, for receiving honors, or for being "Stars of the Week."
>
> Though not strictly letters, *news releases* might be used in conjunction with awards activities as a means of public congratulations.
>
> *Teams* might be congratulated for winning awards or for their performances in state tournaments.
>
> A *Coach* might be congratulated for being selected Coach of the Year.
>
> *Individuals* who choose to retire might also be congratulated for this life change.

Congratulations Letter 3.1
TEACHER, STUDENT WORK DISPLAY

Elementary or Secondary

(Date)

(Name)

(Address)

Dear (Name):

Congratulations on the outstanding exhibition of student (Description) work at the (Event). It was an excellent display. I'm certain that the students, their parents, and our community members enjoyed the display also.

Thank you for making the exhibition possible.

Sincerely,

Principal

Congratulations Letter 3.2
TEACHER, AWARD

Elementary or Secondary

(Date)

(Name)

(Address)

Dear (Name):

Congratulations on winning the (Name of Award) Award. We realize that this award is given to only one educator in the nation each year. Because of your outstanding contributions to the field of (Subject) education, you were selected from all the applicants.

Your teaching talents are clearly recognized by all who have had the chance to work with you. You certainly deserve this national honor.

It is a pleasure to have you as a teacher at (Name of School) School.

Sincerely,

Principal

Congratulations Letter 3.3
TEACHER, ELECTION TO OFFICE

Elementary or Secondary

(Date)

(Name)

(Address)

Dear (Name):

Congratulations on your election to the (Description). We look forward to your leadership in this new position. If I can assist you in any way, please let me know.

Sincerely,

Principal

Congratulations Letter 3.4
TEACHER, DEGREE

Elementary or Secondary

(Date)

(Name)

(Address)

Dear (Name):

Congratulations on completing your master's degree. This is a truly noteworthy accomplishment. The great thing about an academic degree is that you never stop using it!

Congratulations on your achievement.

Sincerely,

Principal

Congratulations Letter 3.5
TEACHER OR STAFF, BIRTH OF CHILD

Elementary or Secondary

(Date)

(Name)

(Address)

Dear (Name):

Congratulations on the birth of your (Son/Daughter), (Name). (He/She) will undoubtedly be a spectacular addition to your household. We look forward to meeting (Him/Her) soon.

Sincerely,

Principal

Congratulations Letter 3.6
TEACHER, PROMOTION

Elementary or Secondary

(Date)

(Name)

(Address)

Dear (Name):

Congratulations on your promotion to (Position) at (Name of School) School. This is a great tribute to your ability. I know you will do an excellent job.

Your leadership and organizational skills will serve you well in this new position. Your ability to get along with staff, students, and parents will also be an asset. Best wishes in your new position!

Sincerely,

Principal

TEACHER, STUDENT ACHIEVEMENT

Elementary or Secondary

(Date)

(Name)

(Address)

Dear (Name):

Congratulations to you and your students on the students' recent performance on their tests. I know that you and the students worked very hard to improve the scores in (Subject) and (Subject). This is a major academic accomplishment.

Congratulations on the super effort!

Sincerely,

Principal

Congratulations Letter 3.8
PARENT(S) OR FAMILY OF TEACHER, TEACHER'S AWARD

Elementary or Secondary

(Date)

(Name)

(Address)

Dear (Name):

I am pleased to inform you that (Teacher's Name) has been awarded the (Name of Award) for the (Year) school year. The (Name of Award) will be presented on (Date) at (Time).

(Name) truly deserves this award. (He/She) is an excellent teacher who always keeps students' needs foremost in (His/Her) efforts.

I would like you to attend the award ceremony that will be held in conjunction with the annual (Name of Conference) on (Day), (Date), at (Time) at the (Name of Room at Conference) in (City).

Congratulations on (Name's) accomplishments. Please call me if you have any questions about the event.

Sincerely,

Principal

Congratulations Letter 3.9
PARENT(S), STUDENT AWARD

Secondary

(Date)

(Name)

(Address)

Dear (Name):

Congratulations! (Name of student) has won the most-improved-student award for (Year). (Name of Student)'s grade point average increased from (GPA) to (GPA). Also, (Name of student) had perfect attendance, was on time for every class, and had no disciplinary referrals during (Year). (Name of student) is making great progress at (Name of School) School. As a reward for (Name of Student)'s achievement, (He/She) will receive (Reward).

We recognize that you played a major role in (Name of Student)'s success, and we appreciate your assistance.

Sincerely,

Principal

PARENT(S), STUDENT GPA

Secondary

(Date)

(Name)

(Address)

Dear (Name):

We are very pleased that your (Son/Daughter), (Name of Student), achieved a perfect 4.0 grade point average during the (Year) school year.

(Name of Student)'s name will be displayed on the special "4.0" plaque in the (Room of the School). We hope you will stop by to see it.

(Name of Student)'s hard work and your support are greatly appreciated.

Sincerely,

Principal

Congratulations Letter 3.11
PARENT(S), STUDENT MENTION IN NEWS

Elementary or Secondary

(Date)

(Name)

(Address)

Dear (Name):

Enclosed is a copy of the article and photo of (Name of Student). We thought you might like to have an extra copy. This is a fine tribute to (Name of Student)'s accomplishments.

Sincerely,

Principal

Congratulations Letter 3.12
PARENT(S), STUDENT SCHOLARSHIP

Secondary

(Date)

(Name)

(Address)

Dear (Name):

Great news! The (Name of Business Company) has awarded your (Son/Daughter), (Name of Student), a (Name of Scholarship) scholarship for graduating with a (GPA) grade point average and for having four years of perfect attendance in high school. I know that you are proud of (Student's name) accomplishments.

Congratulations and best wishes for (Student name's) continued success!

Sincerely,

Principal

Congratulations Letter 3.13
PARENT(S), STUDENT CONTEST WINNER

Elementary or Secondary

(Date)

(Name)

(Address)

Dear (Name):

We understand that (Name of Student) recently won the (Name) Contest. This is a wonderful accomplishment since more than (Number) students from throughout the United States entered the contest.

(Name of Student)'s selection is certainly a reflection of (His/Her) accomplishments as a (Description).

Sincerely,

Principal

Congratulations Letter 3.14
STUDENT, AWARD WINNER (1)

Elementary or Secondary

(Date)

(Name)

(Address)

Dear (Name):

Congratulations! You are the winner of the (Name of Award) Award. Among the accomplishments that contributed to your selection for this award were (Accomplishments). You certainly deserve this honor!

Sincerely,

Principal

Congratulations Letter 3.15
STUDENT, AWARD WINNER (2)

Elementary or Secondary

(Date)

(Name)

(Address)

Dear (Name):

Congratulations on winning the (Name of Award). Your fine work is reflected in this achievement. This is a truly remarkable accomplishment.

Congratulations on a job well done!

Sincerely,

Principal

Congratulations Letter 3.16
STUDENT, AWARD RECIPIENT

Elementary or Secondary

(Date)

(Name)

(Address)

Dear (Name):

We are extremely pleased that you are the recipient of the (Name of Award) Award. You were selected for this honor from a group of (Number) entries. You should be particularly proud of your achievement.

We wish you continued success!

Sincerely,

Principal

Congratulations Letter 3.17
STUDENT, HONOR AWARD

Elementary or Secondary

(Date)

(Name)

(Address)

Dear (Name):

Congratulations on receiving the (Name of Honor) Honor for your quick response during the (Emergency). Your initiative and action in that situation certainly deserve special recognition.

Sincerely,

Principal

Congratulations Letter 3.18
STUDENT, STAR OF THE WEEK

Elementary or Secondary

(Date)

(Name)

(Address)

Dear (Name):

Congratulations on being selected as *Star of the Week*. I look forward to seeing your photo display and listening to your special presentation on (Date).

I hope your week is great!

Sincerely,

Principal

Congratulations Letter 3.19
NEWS RELEASE

Secondary

(Date)

(Name)

(Address)

For Immediate Release

(Name of School) is to present (Name of Award) awards to students on (Date). (Name) will present the awards for outstanding (Name of Awards) to (Number) students at (Time), (Date), in Room (Room Number) of the (Name of Building) building.

Award recipients are (Name), (Name of School) High School; (Name), (Name of School) High School; and (Name), (Name of School) High School. These honorees were selected based on their exceptional (Accomplishments). The students' contributions ranged from (Contributions) to (Contributions).

A reception will follow the award ceremony. The award ceremony and reception are free and open to the public. For information, call (Phone Number).

Congratulations Letter 3.20
TEACHER OR COACH, TEAM AWARD (1)

Elementary or Secondary

(Date)

(Name)

(Address)

Dear (Name):

Congratulations on winning the (Name of Award). You and the (Name of Team) Team have truly earned the prize. I know how hard you and the team worked to achieve this honor.

The trophy for winning the (Award) contest will be on display in Room (Room Number) of (Name of School) School.

Thank you for your efforts on behalf of the students.

Sincerely,

Principal

Congratulations Letter 3.21
TEACHER OR COACH, TEAM AWARD (2)

Secondary

(Date)

(Name)

(Address)

Dear (Name):

Congratulations to you and the (Name of Team) Team on winning first place in the State Tournament. The hard work, dedication, and extra effort certainly paid off.

Congratulations on this major accomplishment!

Sincerely,

Principal

Congratulations Letter 3.22
COACH AWARD

Secondary

(Date)

(Name)

(Address)

Dear (Name):

Congratulations on being selected High School Football Coach of the Year. I know our staff, students, parents, and the community are proud of your selection.

Your hard work, dedication, leadership, and football expertise have been recognized both locally and at the state level.

Congratulations on winning this award!

Sincerely,

Principal

Congratulations Letter 3.23
TEACHER, RETIREMENT

Elementary or Secondary

(Date)

(Name)

(Address)

Dear (Name):

Best wishes on your retirement from (Name of School) School. It is hard to imagine that you are retiring from teaching. You have been such an important part of this school and such a great influence on the lives of our students.

It has always been a pleasure to work with you. You will be greatly missed!

Best wishes as you enjoy your retirement.

Sincerely,

Principal

Congratulations Letter 3.24
STAFF, RETIREMENT

Elementary and Secondary

(Date)

(Name)

(Address)

Dear (Name):

Best wishes on your retirement and thank you for your many contributions to (Name of School) School.

It has been an honor and a pleasure to work with you.

I know the staff and students at (Name of School) School will miss you. You have left behind a fine legacy.

I hope your retirement years will be filled with great happiness. Best wishes to you!

Sincerely,

Principal

4

Sympathy Letters

Letters of sympathy may be the most difficult of all letters to write. The writer is challenged to find appropriate words of comfort. The recipient is often inconsolable. The essential element of the sympathy letter is to say you are sorry for the loss or sadness of a friend or colleague; two examples follow. Simple, direct, and sincere are important guidelines for the expression of sympathy. Sympathy letters are *handwritten*.

Remembering the great qualities or special times with a deceased individual may be thoughtful additions to a sympathy letter. Depending on your relationship, flowers, memorials, or Mass cards may also be appropriate tributes in addition to the sympathy note or card.

Deaths require the expression of sympathy through personal letters and notes.

SYMPATHY LETTER 4.1

Elementary or Secondary

(Date)

Dear (Name):

I was deeply saddened to learn of (Name)'s death. (Name)'s death is a sad loss for you and for (Name)'s friends at (Name of School) School. There really are no words to express this sadness.

Our thoughts are with you.

Sincerely,

SYMPATHY LETTER 4.2

Elementary or Secondary

(Date)

Dear (Name):

We were very sorry to hear about (Name)'s death. The students and staff of (Name of School) extend our deepest sympathy to you on the death of (Name).

You know that you are in our thoughts.

Sincerely,

5

Get-Well Letters

Illness, operations, and accidents are events requiring acknowledgment. The spirit of the notes or letters should be one of care and concern. Reminding individuals that they are in your thoughts is the essence of the message. Occasions for get-well letters include the following:

Accidents are occasions that require notes of sadness and concern for the individual or the family of the individual.

Surgery or illness are events that require a letter or note of concern for the individual or the family.

Get-Well Letter 5.1
ACCIDENT

Elementary or Secondary

(Date)

Dear (Name):

We were all sorry to hear the news about your accident. (Name) called to tell us that you had (Description).

We look forward to your recovery and your return to school. You will be missed!

Sincerely,

Get-Well Letter 5.2
SURGERY (1)

Elementary or Secondary

(Date)

Dear (Name):

We are pleased to hear that your surgery was successful. (Name) told us that you will be in the hospital for (Number) days and that the doctors believe that you should be home by (Date).

We miss you at (Name of School) School and look forward to your return.

Sincerely,

Get-Well Letter 5.3
SURGERY (2)

Elementary or Secondary

(Date)

Dear (Name):

It was wonderful news to hear that your surgery is over and you will be coming home soon. I hope that your recovery is swift. I look forward to seeing you soon!

Sincerely,

Get-Well Letter 5.4
FAMILY ILLNESS

Elementary or Secondary

(Date)

Dear (Name):

I am sorry to learn that (Name) is in the hospital. This must be a very difficult time for you. I sincerely hope that (Name) will make a complete recovery. If I can help in any way, please call me.

Sincerely,

6

Welcome Letters

Welcome letters can set the tone for a school. These letters provide a positive dimension to new experiences, new programs, and meeting new people. A written welcome can ease a transition and provide information that makes the new situation less stressful and less intimidating. These letters are the extras that help make schools welcoming places. The following welcome letters might be sent:

Students might be welcomed to school at the beginning of a new school year.

Parents might be welcomed to a new school year. Parent welcome letters often include important information about the start of the school year, such as announcements of Open House dates and times. New faculty members may also be introduced to parents in the letter.

Neighbors of the school may deserve a "welcome to the school year" letter. This letter provides a bridge to positive neighborhood cooperation.

Staff welcome-back letters help set a positive tone for a new school year. They can also provide important school opening information. Staff letters can be used to introduce new staff members and also to greet new members of the school team. "Welcome back" letters to staff should convey enthusiasm for a new school year and positive regard for the staff.

Welcome Letter 6.1
STUDENT

Elementary

(Date)

(Name)

(Address)

Dear (Student Name):

Welcome to (Grade) grade! I'm looking forward to the start of the school year. You'll have a great time in (Teacher's Name) class. We have some special "welcome back" activities planned for the first week of school that I'm sure you'll enjoy.

See you next week!

Sincerely,

Principal

Welcome Letter 6.2
PARENT(S) (1)

Elementary

(Date)

(Name)

(Address)

Dear (Name):

Welcome to (Name of School) School. All of us at (Name of School) are anticipating another exciting year.

Joining the (Name of School) this year are (Names of New Faculty), (Subjects), (Grades).

FIRST DAY

The first day of school is (Date).

SCHOOL HOURS

School hours effective (Date):

8:55 a.m.–3:30 p.m. for all kindergarten through Grade 6 students.

ATTENDANCE AND TARDINESS

When absences or tardies occur, parents should notify the school office by calling (Phone Number).

LUNCHES

School lunches will cost (Dollar Amount) per day. Children may either buy a lunch ticket for (Period of Time) or pay (Dollar Amount) in the lunchroom each day. Lunch tickets may be purchased on the first day of school, (Date). Children may bring a cold lunch and buy a carton of milk if they desire.

Please refer to the information in the packet regarding free and reduced lunch and breakfast qualifications.

BREAKFAST

The breakfast program will begin (Day) of the week, (Date). Breakfast is served from (Time) to (Time). Children may buy a breakfast ticket good for (Length of Time) for (Dollar Amount).

OPEN HOUSE

Open House will be held (Day of the Week), (Date) from (Time) to (Time). Class lists will be posted by each room. Please come, find your child's room, and become acquainted with (Teacher's Name).

If you have questions or concerns, feel free to call the school or stop by the office. We will assist you in any way we can!

Sincerely,

Principal

Welcome Letter 6.3
PARENT(S) (2)

Secondary

(Date)

(Name)

(Address)

Dear (Name):

Welcome to (Name of School) School. We are looking forward to another great year! Because you may have questions about the start of the school year, the following information is provided for your assistance:

First Day of School:	(Day of Week), (Date)
School Times:	School starts at (Time) a.m. and ends at (Time) p.m.
Lunch:	Students may purchase a school lunch for (Dollar Amount) or may bring a bag lunch. Students may also deposit money in the computerized banking system to pay for their lunches. Reduced-fee or no-fee school lunches are also available. Information concerning reduced-fee or no-fee lunches is attached to this letter.
Locker Assignment:	Locker assignments may be picked up in (Room Number) on (Date) from (Time) to (Time).
Class Schedules:	May be picked up in (Room Number) on (Date) from (Time) to (Time).
Supplies:	Teachers will distribute supply lists.

Also included with this letter is a list of telephone numbers and dates of upcoming events.

We hope the enclosed materials are helpful to you.

Sincerely,

Principal
Enclosures

Welcome Letter 6.4
PARENT(S), INFORMATION SHEET

Secondary

Listed below are important telephone numbers:

— Athletic office

— Attendance office:

— Counselor's office:

— Principal's office

Events

— Open House   (Date)

— Parent Conference Days   (Dates)

— First Quarter Report Card   (Date)

— First Football Game   (Date)

— First Cross Country Meet   (Date)

— First Volleyball Contest   (Date)

Enclosures

— Student Activity Calendar

— Student Handbook

— Reduced-Fee and No-Fee School Lunch Guidelines

Welcome Letter 6.5
PARENT(S) (3)

Secondary

(Date)

(Name)

(Address)

Dear (Name):

Welcome to (Name of School) School!

We are excited about the first day of school, (Date).

We would like all students and families to come to (Name of School), pick up their class schedules, find their classrooms, and meet their teachers at Open House on (Date).

Hot lunches will be served on the first day of school. The cost is (Dollar Amount) per meal. Money can be deposited into lunch accounts during Open House and every school day between (Time) and (Time) a.m. in the school cafeteria. All checks should be made payable to (Name of School). Students may also pay for their meals as they go through the line. Free and reduced-priced meals will be available to families who qualify. An application for free or reduced-price meals is enclosed in this packet. If your family qualifies for either free or reduced-priced meals, please complete the form and return it to the office *before* the first day of school or at Open House. *The school office cannot loan money.*

Please call if your (Son/Daughter) will be absent or tardy. Parents should call (Phone Number) between (Time) and (Time) a.m.

We look forward to a great year, and we hope to see you at Open House!

Sincerely,

Principal

PARENT(S) (4)

Elementary

(Date)

(Name)

(Address)

Dear (Name):

The (Name of School) School staff welcomes your child to the (Year) school year. The first day of school starts at (Time) on (Day of Week), (Date), and ends at (Time).

On the first day of school, your child should report directly to (His/Her) homeroom (Room Number). For the (Year) school year, a hot lunch will cost (Dollar Amount), or your child may bring a sack lunch.

We look forward to seeing your child(ren) on (Day of the Week), (Date).

Enclosed are the Emergency Information Card and the Student Handbook. Please return the emergency card and the student handbook receipt to school on (Date). Also enclosed is a school calendar.

If you have any concerns about any aspect of your child's schooling, feel free to contact the teacher, a guidance counselor, or me. We welcome your inquiries.

We hope these materials are helpful to you. We look forward to a great school year!

Sincerely,

Principal

Enclosures:
    Emergency Information Card
    Student Handbook
    Calendar

Welcome Letter 6.7
PARENT(S) (5)

Kindergarten

(Date)

(Name)

(Address)

Dear (Name):

I hope you have enjoyed many summer activities! I hope, too, that your child is excited about coming to school on (Date).

Please have your child wear the enclosed name tag the first day of school. This is especially important if your child rides the bus.

Our regular time schedule is

AM Kindergarten	PM Kindergarten
8:45 to 11:30 a.m.	12:00 to 2:45 p.m.

The kindergarten teachers for the (Year) school year are (Name), (Room Number), and (Name), (Room Number).

We look forward to seeing you at Open House on (Date).

Sincerely,

Principal

Welcome Letter 6.8
PARENT(S) (6)

Kindergarten

(Date)

(Name)

(Address)

Dear (Name):

Welcome to (Name of school) kindergarten! We are looking forward to a great year with your child!

Following are the procedures for kindergarten students entering and leaving the school.

Where do kindergarten students enter the building? All kindergarten students enter the building from the (Direction). The teacher will meet children at the door the first few weeks of school.

Where do kindergarten students wait to be picked up? Kindergarten students are dismissed at (Time) and (Time) from the (Direction) door. The teacher accompanies them to the main sidewalk and *NEVER* leaves them unattended until all children are picked up.

Please call (Phone Number) if you have any questions. We look forward to the start of school!

Sincerely,

Principal

Welcome Letter 6.9
PARENT(S) (7)

Elementary or Secondary

(Date)

(Name)

(Address)

Dear Parents:

This year, as some of you know, we have had a few changes in personnel. Two teachers are new to the faculty.

(Identify the new teachers and provide brief biographies)

We are happy to welcome these new members. All are well qualified in their teaching disciplines, and I am sure they will enhance our fine faculty.

Sincerely,

Principal

Welcome Letter 6.10
NEIGHBORS

Elementary or Secondary

(Date)

(Name)

(Address)

Dear (Name):

The academic year for our students will start on (Day of the Week), (Date). The school day begins at (Time) a.m. and ends at (Time) p.m. With school buses and cars dropping off and picking up students, these are peak traffic times around (Name of School) School.

As in the past, we will attempt to keep the neighborhood clean. As you know, tips from neighbors can help us to deter suspicious activities. If you suspect problems, please call our office at (Phone Number) during the school day or call the Police Department at (Phone Number) after school hours.

Open House will be held on (Date). We hope you will stop by!

Sincerely,

Principal

Welcome Letter 6.11
STAFF (1)

Elementary or Secondary

(Date)

(Name)

(Address)

Dear (Name):

Welcome back to school. I hope you have had a great summer vacation. Our job at (Name of School) School is to help educate students. That task requires a real team effort. To begin building our team, we will have our first staff meeting of the school year on (Date) from (Time) to approximately (Time), in the school auditorium.

Lunch will be served in the cafeteria at 11:30 a.m.

During the afternoon, you can use your time to prepare for the opening of school.

Our program is what it is because of the dedicated educators such as you who work at our school.

I look forward to working with you and seeing you soon.

Sincerely,

Principal

Welcome Letter 6.12
STAFF (2)

Elementary

(Date)

(Name)

(Address)

Dear (Name):

Summer vacations provide time for rest and relaxation. I hope you are rejuvenated and ready for the start of a new year at (Name of School).

As the beginning of the new year approaches, I look forward to opening day. Opening day offers excitement and promise for educators and students alike. When our students return to school on (Date), we will have a great opportunity to make a difference in their lives. Our array of talents, as faculty, have far-reaching effects toward establishing a rich and stimulating learning environment for the students of (Name of School).

Joining the (Name of School) team this year are: (Name), Grades (Number); (Name), Grades (Number); and (Name), Grades (Number). I want to extend a welcome to our newly hired faculty on behalf of the staff and students of (Name of School).

To all of you *Welcome Back!* I look forward to the (Year) school year and envision a year filled with excitement and many reasons to celebrate.

Please note the following meeting times:

(Day of Week), (Date), (Time), (Name of Meeting).

(Day of Week), (Date), (Time), (Name of Meeting).

See you then!

Sincerely,

Principal

Welcome Letter 6.13
STAFF (3)

Elementary

(Date)

(Name)

(Address)

Dear Staff:

I am looking forward to the new school year and hope you are too. Our first official day back is (Date).

Our first staff meeting of the year will be held on (Date). We will have a continental breakfast available at (Time). The meeting will start at (Time). I'm enclosing a calendar and handbook with this letter for your information.

I look forward to seeing you soon!

Sincerely,

Principal
Enclosures

Welcome Letter 6.14
STAFF (4)

Elementary or Secondary

(Date)

(Name)

(Address)

Dear (Name):

Welcome to (Name of School) School. The staff, parents, and students feel that our school is the best in the state. We've received national recognition for student performance as well as for the outstanding teaching by our faculty.

We look forward to working with you at the teacher orientation program on (Date) at (Name of School) School. The agenda for the orientation program follows:

    8:00 to 8:30 a.m.   Continental breakfast

    8:30 to 8:45 a.m.   Welcome by the principal and staff

    8:45 to 12:00 p.m. New teacher orientation

    12:00 to 1:00 p.m. Lunch in school cafeteria

    1:00 to 3:00 p.m.   Class preparation

    3:00 to 3:30 p.m.   Meeting with principal, mentors

At the orientation, you will receive a staff handbook, curriculum guides, teacher textbooks, your room keys, and other materials.

Lunch will be served at 12 noon. At that time, your mentor teacher (Name) will join us. You and your mentor teacher will be able to work together during the afternoon preparing your classroom. Afterward, we will meet at 3:00 p.m. to discuss any questions you may have.

I look forward to seeing you soon.

Sincerely,

Principal

Welcome Letter 6.15
STAFF INFORMATION SHEET

Elementary or Secondary

(Date)

(Name)

(Address)

Dear (Name):

Staff Update: We welcome our new teacher, (Name)

Positions yet to be filled: (Positions)

Postcards: As most of you are aware, each year teachers send postcards to students in their homerooms to welcome them to the upcoming school year. This activity is a tradition at (Name of School). Labels for the postcards may be picked up in the office after (Date) or you may hand address them. Teachers, please write out an extra card or two in case you have a new student. Please include your room number on the postcards. They are due (Date). Thank you!

First Day Back for Teachers: (Date)

Open House will be (Date)

Sincerely,

Principal

Welcome Letter 6.16
STAFF (5)

Elementary

(Date)

(Name)

Dear Staff:

I have the highest regard for the dedication, diverse talents, and skills of our staff and the effects they have on our students. I am impressed daily with your caring ways for students and staff.

I look forward to the (Year) school year and the exciting opportunities it will bring.

Sincerely,

Principal

7

Information and Procedures Letters, Memos, Forms, and Announcements

Information and procedures letters provide direction and give guidance. Their ultimate aim is to provide clarity, eliminate confusion, and answer potential questions. Letters sent by the principal should be timely so that they are of maximum assistance to the school community. Information and procedures letters might be sent for the following reasons:

Student safety concerns may require the sharing of information and procedural directions. Bus safety, fire safety, stranger danger, emergencies, and field trips are instances when letters to parents may be required.

Grading, achievement tests, and *athletics* may necessitate letters to parents or guardians.

Ordering supplies, gathering items for daily newsletters, preparing teaching portfolios, upcoming changes, or *preparing news releases* are some of the reasons staff members might receive information or procedures letters.

Summer school, graduation, and the *end of the school year* are other events that require information and procedural letters for students, parents, and staff.

Information and Procedures Letter 7.1
PARENT(S), SAFETY (1)

Elementary

(Date)

(Name)

(Address)

Dear Parents and Guardians:

As you may have seen on television or heard on the radio, the police are seeking information about the driver of a van who approached children on their way to school this morning. The children responded appropriately and are safe. This is the third such incident that has occurred in our community in recent weeks. The police are investigating these incidents and will be monitoring the streets around the school.

This may be a good time to discuss safety issues with your children, particularly if they walk to and from school. Please review safety procedures with your children.

Sincerely,

Principal

Information and Procedures Letter 7.2
PARENT(S), SAFETY (2)

Elementary

(Date)

(Name)

(Address)

Dear (Name):

As you may have already heard, school bus (Number), which your child rides, was involved in a minor accident at (Address) on (Date), at approximately (Time). I am pleased to report that no child was seriously injured.

If you want more information about this accident, please contact (School Office) at (Phone Number).

Sincerely,

Principal

Information and Procedures Letter 7.3
PARENT(S), SAFETY (3)

Elementary or Secondary

(Date)

(Name)

(Address)

Dear (Name):

As you may have heard, the fire department arrived at our school at approximately (Time) today. A fire was caused in the (Place) by (Means). All students and staff were safely evacuated.

Students and staff were out of the building for approximately 30 minutes. No major damage occurred to the school, and no one was injured. If you have any questions about the situation, please call me at (Phone Number).

Sincerely,

Principal

Information and Procedures Letter 7.4
PARENT(S), FIELD TRIPS

Elementary

(Date)

(Name)

(Address)

Dear (Name):

Field trips are an important part of your child's education. Once again, we ask you to complete the enclosed form granting permission for your child to participate in a field trip.

The forms must be filled out, signed, and returned to the school prior to the trip. No student will be allowed on any trip without this signed and completed form. Teachers will not be allowed to make exceptions to this rule.

Thank you for your assistance.

Sincerely,

Principal

Information and Procedures Letter and Form 7.5
PARENT(S), EMERGENCIES

Elementary

(Date)

(Name)

(Address)

Dear Parent or Guardian:

If severe weather or an emergency causes the early closing of school, we need to make sure that all students arrive at their destinations safely.

On the following form, please indicate what your child should do if school is dismissed early.

Thank you for your assistance in providing this information.

Sincerely,

Principal

- -

Please detach and return to school by (Date).

Emergency Instructions for

Student's Name _____ Room Number _____

_____ Go directly home

_____ Go to day care provider

_____ Remain at school until picked up

_____ Take school bus (if your child is transported by bus each day)

_____ Other_____

_____   _____

Parent or Guardian Signature   Date

Information and Procedures Letter and Form 7.6
PARENT(S), GRADING PERIOD

Secondary

(Date)

(Name)

(Address)

Dear (Name):

The first grading period ends on (Date). We report student averages at this time to allow students and parents an opportunity to review progress.

If you are not satisfied with the progress indicated by this report, there are still three weeks before the end of the first grading period. Improvement is still possible.

Subject _____ Current Average_____

Comments _____

Please sign this report and return it to the subject teacher. If you have questions or concerns about the progress described in this report, please call (Name), the teacher, at (Phone Number).

Sincerely,

Principal

Parent's Signature _____

Information and Procedures Letter 7.7
PARENT(S), ACHIEVEMENT TESTS

Elementary

(Date)

(Name)

(Address)

Dear (Name):

Last (Month), the (Name of Test) Achievement Test was administered to your child at (Name of School) School.

This test is used as a tool to help measure the academic progress of your child and to discover strengths and weaknesses that could help us in meeting your child's educational needs.

Enclosed you will find a copy of your child's achievement test results. A summary report of the performance of all students in the district as well as students throughout the United States is also enclosed.

If you would like to discuss these results with (Name of Student's Teacher), please call (Phone Number). We hope this information is useful to you.

Sincerely,

Principal

Information and Procedures Letter and Form 7.8
PARENT(S), ATHLETICS

Secondary

(Date)

(Name)

(Address)

Dear (Name):

Please sign the following form if you received and reviewed the athletic handbook and agree to the statement below. To be eligible to participate in interscholastic athletics, your child must return this form to the coach by (Time). The coach must also receive a completed physical form.

We have received a copy of the (Name of School) School's Handbook for Athletics. We understand the stated policies, rules, and regulations and intend to abide by them.

I give permission for _____ to participate
(Student's name)

in _____.
(Sport)

_____   _____

Signature of Parent or Guardian   Date

_____   _____

Signature of Student   Date

Information and Procedures Letter 7.9
PARENT(S), ATHLETICS

Secondary

(Date)

(Name)

(Address)

Dear (Name):

This is to inform you that (Name of Student) is academically ineligible for all activities in accordance with (Page in Academic Handbook).

Academic Eligibility

The (Name of School) School has the following four requirements for participation in activities:

1. All participants must be in grades (Numbers), in regular attendance, and taking a minimum of (Number) credit hours in (Number) classes.
2. If a participant is taking (Number) credit hours, he or she must be passing (Number) credit hours to be eligible.
3. Eligibility will be determined each grading period.
4. If a student is not passing (Number) of (Number) classes during a grading period, then he or she will remain ineligible until the student's grades are high enough to be removed from the ineligible list.

If you have any questions, please call me at (Phone Number).

Sincerely,

Principal

Information and Procedures Memo 7.10
STAFF, SUPPLIES

Elementary or Secondary

(Date)

MEMORANDUM

TO: Staff

FROM: (Name), Principal

RE: Ordering Supplies

You might want to order supplies early to avoid the end-of-semester rush.

Please note the following six points:

1. Supply orders are due (Date).
2. Use the requisition forms. Be sure to list the vendor on the form.
3. Please use the approved vendor catalogs.
4. The catalogs are in (School Office).
5. Figure in the cost of shipping and handling on orders from vendors. Make sure to check your figures.
6. The following items will be ordered by the office: printed forms, report cards, letterhead, and envelopes of all sizes.

If you have any questions regarding your orders, please check with (Name) or me.

Thanks.

Information and Procedures Form 7.11
TEACHERS AND STAFF, DAILY NEWS

Elementary

DAILY NEWS   Date _____

Please post items of interest to the staff! We'll distribute the news before lunch.

_____

_____

_____

_____

_____

_____

_____

_____

_____

_____

_____

_____

_____

_____

Staff Absences: _____

_____

_____

Dates to Remember: _____

_____

Information and Procedures Memo 7.12
TEACHER, PORTFOLIO PREPARATION

Elementary or Secondary

(Date)

MEMORANDUM

TO: (Name)

FROM: (Name), Principal

RE: Portfolio Preparation

As you prepare your portfolios as part of the annual assessment process, please consider providing evidence of the following:

- Professional associations you belong to and your specific activities within the associations
- Indicators of teaching effectiveness (student evaluations, parent evaluations, examples of student work, student honors related to your instruction, self-assessments based on professional goals)
- Student organizations you provide leadership for and the students' accomplishments
- Professional development activities you have participated in this year, including courses, workshops, conferences, seminars, readings, visits to other sites, and so forth
- Honors and awards you have received this year
- Grant applications that have been submitted or funded
- Special projects

Please submit your portfolio before our meeting on (Date).

Thanks for your help!

Information and Procedures Letter 7.13
PARENT(S), UPCOMING CHANGES

Elementary or Secondary

(Date)

(Name)

(Address)

Dear (Name):

I have scheduled a special meeting to provide information and answer questions you might have about the changes planned for the school in the future. My purpose is to provide you with as much information as I can. You deserve to hear information directly from me.

We will do everything we can to address the changes in a sensitive and supportive manner.

I look forward to meeting with you on (Day of Week), (Date), at (Time). I hope you will attend.

Sincerely,

Principal

Information and Procedures Handout 7.14
TEACHER, NEWS RELEASE

Elementary or Secondary

PREPARING A NEWS RELEASE FOR THE PRESS

Keep the following in mind as you craft any news release:

How will I "grab" the reporter's attention?

Did I answer the who, what, when, and where questions?

Does the information appear in order of importance?

Did I keep it brief and to the point?

Are the facts and spelling accurate?

Did I avoid jargon and technical terms?

Information and Procedures Letter 7.15
PARENT(S) OR GUARDIAN(S), SUMMER SCHOOL

Elementary

(Date)

(Name)

(Address)

Dear (Name):

Previously, we had discussed the possibility of (Name of Student)'s repeating the (Number) grade. When a student does not make adequate progress, grade repeating becomes necessary.

The alternative is for (Name) to attend summer school in (Month) and (Month). Successful completion of summer school will result in promotion to (Number) grade.

Summer school meets (Days of the Week) from (Time) to (Time) at (Name of School) School. The fee for summer school is (Dollar Amount).

To register for summer school, please contact (Name) at (Phone Number).

Sincerely,

Principal

Information and Procedures Letter 7.16
PARENT(S) OR GUARDIAN(S), GRADUATION

Secondary

(Date)

(Name)

(Address)

Dear (Name):

The high school class of (Year) is scheduled to graduate on (Day of the Week), (Date), at (Time) at (Place). The public is invited to attend the ceremony.

Each senior must arrive at (Place) by (Time). Graduates only will assemble in (Place) before the graduation ceremony.

The (Place) will be open for seating at (Time). Individuals with disabilities will have access to seating in (Area).

Caps and gowns will be worn for graduation. Caps and gowns can be picked up on (Day of Week), (Date), from (Time) to (Time) in the (School Office).

Graduation is a formal event. Proper behavior is expected of all in attendance. Do not bring noisemakers or other distracting items into the (Place).

A professional photographer will take a picture of each graduate as the diploma is presented. A video of the graduation ceremony is also being produced. The picture and video will be available for purchase from the professional photographer. Personal pictures may also be taken in the specially designated area near the stage. Please do not disrupt the ceremony when taking pictures.

Diplomas will be available immediately following the ceremony in (Room Number). Students who have not completed all requirements for graduation will not receive a diploma.

If you have questions about graduation, please call (School Office) at (Phone Number).

Sincerely,

Principal

Information and Procedures Handout 7.17
STUDENT, GRADUATION

Secondary

SENIORS END-OF-THE-YEAR REMINDERS

1. *Commencement Practice:* Practice for commencement will be held on (Date) from (Time) to (Time) in (Location).

2. *Lockers:* Locks must be turned in at the office. If a lock is not returned, there is a (Dollar Amount) fine. Seniors will be expected to clean their lockers prior to the last day of school, (Date).

3. *Last Day of School:* The last attendance day for seniors is (Date). Make sure that your class work is finished, all fines are paid, and that your record is clear before this time.

4. *Senior Responsibilities:* Any senior who has not fulfilled *ALL* responsibilities will not be awarded a diploma at commencement. Responsibilities include books checked in, fines paid, academic work completed, and locks returned.

5. *Commencement:* The (Name of School) High School (Year) Commencement is scheduled at (Location) at (Time), (Day of the Week), (Date). Plan to arrive at the (Location) by (Time) that day. Caps and gowns must be worn.

Information and Procedures Letter 7.18
STUDENT, END OF YEAR

Secondary

(Date)

(Student Name)

(Address)

Dear (Student Name):

Congratulations on the completion of the (Year) year at (Name of School).

School Calendar: The (Next Year) Year School Calendar is enclosed. The first day of student attendance will be (Day of the Week), (Date).

Changes in Address: If your permanent mailing address changes, please notify us immediately. You will want to receive the special summer mailings as well as your (Next Year) Class Schedule.

Reminder to Athletes: Physical examinations are valid for one school year only. You might want to schedule appointments for your physical exams now. No athletic equipment will be issued or participation of any type allowed until physical examination and parent consent forms are completed. These forms may be obtained in the (School Office) Office throughout the summer.

Summer Office Hours: The (School Office) Office will be open Monday through Friday from (Time) to (Time) throughout the summer. If you need information or help, please come in or call us at (Phone Number).

Best wishes for a pleasant summer.

Sincerely,

Principal

Information and Procedures Letter 7.19
PARENT(S), END OF YEAR

Elementary

(Date)

(Name)

(Address)

Dear (Name):

I'm sure you'll want to join me in saying *Thank you, (Name)*. A huge thank you goes to (Name) for donating (Item) for the (Name of School). Congratulations to (Name), (Name), (Name), and (Name) the winners of the (Prize).

Next Year's Plans: Please notify the office (Position) if your child will *not* be attending (Name of School) next year.

Field Day: Our field day is scheduled for (Day of the Week), (Date), (Time). Please contact the office if you would be able to volunteer for one or two hours to run a game or activity. The rain date is (Date).

Year Account: Our cafeteria staff will be working with students to use up the balance in their (Year) accounts. If your child's account is depleted, with only a few school days left, we suggest you send cash.

At the end of the school year, any (Type) accounts that contain less than $2.00 will be automatically cleared without a refund. Accounts with a balance over $2.00 will have refunds available on request in the school office through (Date), then in the Accounting Department at (Name of District) District Office until (Date). Any unclaimed balances in the accounts will revert back to the (Name of Account).

Dates to remember

(Date)	Concert _____
(Date)	PTO Meeting _____
(Date)	No School _____
(Date)	Field Day _____
(Date)	No School _____
(Date)	Field Day (Rain Date)_____
(Date)	Report Cards Sent Home _____
(Date)	Last Day of School _____

Change of Address: Please notify the office of any address changes so that you will receive summer mailings promptly.

Sincerely,

Principal

Information and Procedures Form 7.20
STUDENT, END OF YEAR

Secondary

CHECKOUT

Student End of Year

Name _____

This form is to be completed and turned into the principal's office before you are cleared for promotion or graduation. This form is due by _____.

Period	*Class*	*Books Checked In*	*Book Fines Paid*	*Work Completed*	*Teacher Initials*
Period 1					
Period 2					
Period 3					
Period 4					
Period 5					
Period 6					
Period 7					
Period 8					

Information and Procedures Memo 7.21
TEACHER, END OF YEAR (1)

Elementary or Secondary

(Date)

TO: Teaching Staff

FROM: (Name), Principal

RE: Next year's calendar, last days of school, and staff checkout

NEXT YEAR'S CALENDAR

If you have any special events planned for next year, please submit the proposed date before you leave for the summer. We will prepare a master calendar for next year so that when you are planning a special activity, you will know if it conflicts with any other activity.

LAST DAYS OF SCHOOL

Let's make the last days of this school year as positive for students as this school year has been for them already. Please be aware of the guidelines for showing movies, and make sure any movie you show is part of your overall curriculum plan. I will be reminding students about nuisance items during the last days of school. Please help with these reminders and be on the lookout also for any inappropriate items. Turn them into the office if anything is found or taken from a student.

HALL SUPERVISION

Please help with hallway supervision and be as visible as possible to the students during these last (Number) days of school.

STAFF CHECKOUT

Staff will need to be completely ready to check out on (Date). We will provide more information about checkout as soon as possible.

Information and Procedures Form 7.22
TEACHER, END OF YEAR (2)

Secondary

FACULTY CHECK OUT

Tasks		*Initials*
1. All grades recorded on the report cards		
Checked by	_____	_____
2. Books, audio, and video materials returned to the library		
Checked by Librarian		_____
3. Grade books turned into the building principal		
Checked by	_____	_____
4. Classrooms clean—Checked by building principal		_____
a. No pictures or posters on bulletin boards or walls		_____
b. Book shelves clean and emptied		_____
c. Desk clean and everything put away		_____
5. Inventories turned into the building principal		
Checked by	_____	_____
6. All keys returned and verified against key list		
Checked by	_____	_____
7. Room repairs list turned into_____		
Checked by	_____	_____
8. Athletic inventory turned into athletic director		
Checked by	_____	_____
9. Athletic budget turned into the athletic director		
Checked by	_____	_____

10. Summer address: Name:_____

Telephone Number: _____

Check out time _____, _____

Information and Procedures Form 7.23
TEACHER, END OF YEAR (3)

Secondary

TEACHER'S SIGN-OUT SHEET

Name:_____

1. Grade book in the principal's office   _____

2. Room cleaned   _____

3. Inventory turned into the principal's office   _____

4. Keys and key identification list returned to _____   _____

5. Repair list turned in to _____   _____

6. Coaches: All equipment and inventory turned into athletic director   _____

8

Discipline Letters and Forms

Discipline is an important aspect of a principal's role. Letters and documentation of discipline concerns are often prescribed by school district policies and contained in school district policy manuals. In serious instances, state statutes may determine a principal's response to a discipline problem. A school district attorney may also be involved in responding to discipline concerns.

Documentation of discipline problems is an important administrative responsibility. Addressing school discipline concerns requires an accurate accounting of the sources and types of discipline infractions. Letters and documentation of discipline problems might include the following:

Discipline referrals are reported to parents and documented in the principal's office.

Student discipline interventions may be documented in a discipline log.

Tardies, discipline infractions, and *behavior warnings* are reported to parents and copies of the letters maintained in the appropriate files.

Bus misbehaviors may require letters to parents, and copies of these letters should be placed in an appropriate file.

Student suspensions are accompanied by letters to parents. Copies of suspension letters should be placed in appropriate school files.

Discipline Form 8.1
REFERRAL FORM

Elementary or Secondary

STUDENT DISCIPLINE REFERRAL

Name_____ Grade _____

Date _____ Teacher _____

Referral Initiated by _____

Discipline Problem

A. Student-student   _____
B. Student-staff   _____
C. Violation of school rules   _____
D. Repeated violations of rules or referrals   _____
E. Attendance   _____
F. Bus behavior   _____
G. Other   _____

Parent Contact: *Phone*   *Conference*   *Letter*

Action: _____

_____

Removal from School: Rest of day _____ One or more days _____ Expulsion _____

Comments: _____

_____

_____

Grady, M.L., *124 High-Impact Letters for Busy Principals,* © 2000, Corwin Press, Inc.

Discipline Form 8.2
STUDENT BEHAVIOR RECORD

Elementary or Secondary

OFFICE INTERVENTION LOG

Name:_____

Date	Class	Behavior	Consequence(s)	Parent Contact[a]

a. Parent contact: 1 = phone; 2 = letter, report; 3 = conference

Discipline Letter 8.3
PARENT(S), TARDIES

Elementary or Secondary

(Date)

(Name)

(Address)

Dear (Name):

(Name of Student) has been tardy to class (Number) times since the beginning of the school year. Although we realize that emergencies occur on occasion, we expect students to arrive at school on time. It is important for (Name) to receive all the instruction that is available to (Him/Her). Also, it is disruptive for the class and instruction when a student arrives late. It is often difficult for a child to enter a room when (He/She) is late. Currently, the state statute regarding tardiness states the following: (Statute).

We would appreciate your assistance in helping (Name) arrive at school on time.

Sincerely,

Principal

Discipline Letter 8.4
PARENT(S), INFRACTION

Elementary and Secondary

(Date)

(Name)

(Address)

Dear (Name):

Your child has a discipline infraction of (Description of Infraction). This is the (Number) offense. As per the (Name of School) manual, the consequences will be (Description of Consequences).

If you have any questions about this situation, please refer to page (Number) of the (Name of School) manual.

Sincerely,

Principal

Discipline Letter 8.5
PARENT(S), WARNING

Elementary and Secondary

(Date)

(Name)

(Address)

Dear (Name):

During the past few days, several students have acted or made comments that have been inappropriate. Your (Son/Daughter), (Name), has acted in this manner.

The involved students have been told that if similar situations recur, detentions or suspensions from school may be the consequences. The inappropriate behavior and comments may be perceived as sexual harassment and are not tolerated by our school district. Page (Number) of the student handbook provides specific information about district policies.

We would appreciate your assistance in talking with (Name) about this behavior and the potential consequences if the behavior persists.

If you have any questions, please contact me.

Sincerely,

Principal

Discipline Letter 8.6
PARENT(S), BUS MISBEHAVIOR (1)

Elementary

(Date)

(Name)

(Address)

Dear (Name):

Today on the bus, (Name of Student) (Behavior). I reviewed the situation with (Him/Her). (Name of Student) agreed that (He/She) broke a bus rule and was aware of the consequences of (His/Her) actions.

According to district procedures, students who are reported to the principal for misbehavior on the bus will receive a verbal warning and a letter will be sent to the parents following the first offense. If a second offense occurs, however, a two-day suspension of bus privileges may be imposed following parent contact.

Please discuss this incident with (Name of Student), and thank you for your support of our efforts to provide safe transportation for students. If you have questions, please feel free to call me at (Phone Number).

Sincerely,

Principal

cc: Transportation Director
     Bus Driver
     Teacher
     Guidance Counselor
     File

Discipline Letter 8.7
PARENT(S), BUS MISBEHAVIOR (2)

Elementary

(Date)

(Name)

(Address)

Dear (Name):

Your (Son/Daughter), (Name of Student) has been reported for misbehavior on the school bus (Number) times this year. According to the Student Handbook, (Page Number), such referrals result in suspension from riding the school bus. Thus (Name of Student) is suspended from riding the school bus as of (Day of the Week), (Date).

In accordance with (Name of District) School District procedures, it will be necessary for you to meet with (Name of Student), the bus driver, and me before bus-riding privileges can be restored. Please contact me at (Phone Number) to arrange a convenient meeting time.

Sincerely,

Principal

Discipline Letter 8.8
PARENT(S), BUS MISBEHAVIOR (3)

Elementary

(Date)

(Name)

(Address)

Dear (Name):

We regret to inform you that (Name of Student)'s bus-riding privileges have been suspended from (Date) to (Date). When a situation arises that endangers the safety of other students, it is necessary for the school to take appropriate measures to correct it.

The reason or reasons for this suspension of bus privileges are as follows: (Description of Infraction).

If you have any questions, please feel free to call me at (Phone Number).

During the suspension, it is the responsibility of the parents to provide transportation.

Sincerely,

Principal

Discipline Letter 8.9
PARENT(S), SUSPENSION (1)

Elementary or Secondary

(Date)

(Name)

(Address)

Dear (Name):

(Name of Student) has been suspended from classes at (Name of School) School for a period of (Number) days. The suspension will be an in-school suspension and will be served (How Served) through (Date). (Name of Student) is to report to the In-School Suspension Room (Room Number) at (Time) and will be released at (Time).

While on suspension, (Name of Student) will be expected to complete assignments from (His/Her) teachers each day. The class work completed will be returned to the teachers and full credit given.

The suspension is the result of (Name of Student)'s involvement in (Description of Infraction).

If you have questions about this suspension, please call me at (Phone Number).

Sincerely,

Principal

Discipline Letter 8.10
PARENT(S), SUSPENSION (2)

Elementary or Secondary

(Date)

(Name)

(Address)

Dear (Name):

This is to notify you that your child, (Name of Student), has been suspended from (Name of School) School for the following period of time: (Date) through (Date).

The reason for this suspension is (Description of Infraction).

On (Date) at (Time), we require that one or both of you accompany (Name of Student) to school for a short conference. This conference is required before (Name of Student) can be reinstated.

If you have any questions regarding this matter, please call me at (Phone Number).

Sincerely,

Principal

9

Letters Acknowledging Complaints

Acknowledgments should be brief and specific. One simply notes receipt of the complaint and indicates an intention to respond to the complaint as soon as further information is available.

Either written or verbal complaints may be received. The first obligation is to thank the individual for bringing the issue to the principal's attention. Copies of the letter written in response to the complaint should be maintained in appropriate files because complaints may not be easily resolved.

Letters acknowledging complaints may include the following:

Written or verbal complaints should be responded to with letters.

Concerns about book assignments may call for a letter of acknowledgment.

Continuing concerns about their children's education can necessitate letters to parents.

Letter Acknowledging Complaint 9.1
WRITTEN COMPLAINT

Elementary or Secondary

(Date)

(Address)

Dear (Name):

I want you to know that I received your letter dated (Date) concerning (Concern). I appreciate the opportunity to respond to your concern. I will look into the situation and contact you once I have more information.

Sincerely,

Principal

Letter Acknowledging Complaint 9.2
TELEPHONE COMPLAINT

Elementary or Secondary

(Date)

(Address)

Dear (Name):

This is to acknowledge your telephone call of (Date). I appreciate your bringing this issue to my attention. We have begun to inquire about the situation. When we have further information, we will call you.

If you have further concerns, please call us at (Phone Number).

Sincerely,

Principal

Letter Acknowledging Complaint 9.3
BOOK COMPLAINT

Elementary or Secondary

(Date)

(Address)

Dear (Name):

This is to acknowledge receipt of your letter about the (Concern) that your (Son/Daughter) has been using in (His/Her) class.

I understand that you are concerned about (Concern).

Your (Son/Daughter) is excused from reading (Book). (Teacher Name) has been asked to provide (Name of Student) with another story on a different theme, one that you and (Name of Student) will not find objectionable.

We hope this addresses your concern.

Sincerely,

Principal

Letter Acknowledging Complaint 9.4
ONGOING COMPLAINT

Elementary

(Date)

(Address)

Dear (Name):

We received the message you sent yesterday, (Date). We have been in conversation about the perceived problem since (Date). We have met with you several times, exchanged messages, and talked with you by phone. We have also taken steps to ensure that (Describe Solution).

Your recent message indicates that you continue to have concerns. You mentioned that (Concern). Despite repeated requests for (Name of Student) to immediately report such behavior to the adult in charge, we did not learn of the incident until (Name of Student) shared it with me on (Date). We do not tolerate such behavior, and when it occurs, we would like the opportunity to correct it right away. (Name of Student) can help by reporting any incident as soon as it occurs.

I would be pleased to meet with you if that would be helpful.

Sincerely,

Principal

10

Recommendation Letters

Letters of recommendation are written on behalf of individuals you know. The letters should be factual, noting specific skills or abilities of the individual. The focus should be on the individual's accomplishments in relation to the intention of the letter. Letters of recommendation and letters of reference are not synonymous. The letter of recommendation is written to advocate for an individual. The letter of reference documents an individual's employment or enrollment.

A principal has many opportunities to write letters of recommendation such as the following:

Teachers, student teachers, and staff members may request letters of recommendation when they apply for jobs.

Letters may also be written in support of teachers who are nominees for awards.

Students may request letters of recommendation when they seek employment and admission to colleges or universities.

Recommendation Letter 10.1
TEACHER JOB APPLICATION (1)

Elementary or Secondary

(Date)

(Name)

(Address)

Dear (Name):

(Name) has asked me to write a letter of recommendation on (His/Her) behalf. I am happy to do so. (Name) began (His/Her) teaching career at (Name of School) School in (Year). (He/She) has worked here for (Number) years. Presently, (Name) is the chairperson of the (Name of Department) Department working with (Number) other department teachers.

(Name) is an outstanding professional who works hard to make the (Name of Department) Department a model of excellence. (He/She) works well with teachers, students, parents, and administrators. Everyone appreciates (His/Her) knowledge and expertise in education.

(Name) is a leader who brings new and creative projects to the department. (Name of School) School has been fortunate to have a person of (Name)'s qualities working at the school.

I have no doubt that (Name) will continue to be an excellent educator. I highly recommend (Name) for the (Position) position at your school.

If I can supply any further information in support of (Name)'s application, please let me know.

Sincerely,

Principal

Recommendation Letter 10.2
TEACHER JOB APPLICATION (2)

Secondary

(Date)

To Whom It May Concern:

This is a letter of recommendation for (Name). (Name) taught in the (Department) at (Name of School) High School for the past (Number) years. I have found (Name) to be a student-centered teacher. Students ask to be in (His/Her) classes because they find the subject matter interesting and (Name) entertaining. Also, it is apparent (Name) has an excellent rapport with students; that is another reason students want to be in (His/Her) classes.

In addition to (His/Her) effective teaching skills, (Name) gives of (Himself/Herself) outside the classroom. (He/She) sponsors the (Name of Club) Club. With (His/Her) group, (Name) is well organized and works hard to ensure that students have a successful experience.

In conclusion, (Name) has been a very successful teacher at (Name of School), and (He/She) comes with my highest recommendation.

Sincerely,

Principal

Recommendation Letter 10.3
TEACHER JOB APPLICATION (3)

Elementary or Secondary

(Date)

(Name)

(Address)

Dear (Name):

I am writing this letter in support of (Name)'s application for the (Position) position at (Name of School) School.

I have had the opportunity to observe (Name)'s work during the (Number) years while (She/He) taught at (Name of School) School.

(Name) has excellent rapport with students. (Name)'s teaching is challenging and exciting for students. I'm certain (He/She) has copies of (His/Her) evaluations from (Number) years at (Name of School) School that document (His/Her) consistent, excellent teaching.

We are exceptionally sorry that (Name) is moving to (City, State). (He/She) will be truly missed here. I highly recommend (Name) for the (Position) position. If I can answer any questions you might have, please call me at (Phone Number).

Sincerely,

Principal

Recommendation Letter 10.4
STUDENT TEACHER JOB APPLICATION (1)

Elementary or Secondary

(Date)

(Name)

(Address)

Dear (Name):

I am pleased to recommend (Name) for a teaching position in the (Name of School District) School District. (Name) has exceptional skill and ability.

During the (Season) of the (Year) academic year, (Name) was a student teacher at (Name of School). (He/She) taught (Subject) to (Grade) students. (Name) was highly regarded by (His/Her) cooperating teacher. (He/She) worked well with all levels of ability and found ways to challenge all students.

(Name) has tremendous enthusiasm for teaching. Students enjoy (His/Her) classes and work hard to meet (His/Her) expectations. Students were actively involved in (Name)'s classes.

I highly recommend (Name) for the teaching position in your school district. (He/She) will be an excellent addition to your staff.

Sincerely,

Principal

Recommendation Letter 10.5
STUDENT TEACHER JOB APPLICATION (2)

Secondary

(Date)

To Whom It May Concern:

This is a letter of reference for (Name), who student taught at (Name of School) High School from (Year) to (Year). (Name)'s main responsibilities have been with (Subject) and (Subject).

(Name) has done an excellent job with (His/Her) student teaching assignment. (Name) is talented.

In addition, (Name) is dependable, and (He/She) is a hard worker. (Name)'s cooperating teacher, (Name), describes (Name) as highly motivated and effective.

It has been a pleasure to have (Name) student teach at (Name of School) High School this semester. If I can supply any further information in support of (Name)'s application, please let me know.

Sincerely,

Principal

Recommendation Letter 10.6
STAFF JOB APPLICATION

Elementary or Secondary

(Date)

(Name)

(Address)

Dear (Name):

(Name) has asked that I write a letter in support of (His/Her) application for the position of (Position). I am pleased to write on (Name) behalf.

(Name) was employed as a (Position) at (Name of School) School for (Number) years. During that time, (He/She) worked under the supervision of (Name) to organize materials for (Subject). In addition, (He/She) taught (Subject) to small groups of students. (He/She) did an outstanding job. (Name) had excellent rapport with students as well as staff. All staff members respected (Her/Him).

(Name) will be an asset to your school as well as to the school system.

If I can supply any further information in support of (His/Her) application, please let me know.

Sincerely,

Principal

Recommendation Letter 10.7
EDUCATOR AWARD NOMINATION

Elementary or Secondary

(Date)

To The Selection Committee:

Please accept this nomination of (Name) for the (Name of Award) Award. (Name) has taught at (Name of School) for (Number) years. (Name) has been a tremendous positive influence for the students of our school. Throughout (His/Her) career, (Name) has been recognized as an outstanding educator.

(Name) is highly regarded by all teachers. (He/She) is dedicated, thoughtful, and on the cutting edge of the (Course) field. (Name) is frequently called on to make presentations at professional meetings because of (Name)'s expertise. These presentations are represented in the file provided in support of this nomination. (Name)'s leadership in education is clearly demonstrated through (His/Her) career.

It is truly an honor to nominate (Name) for the (Name of Award) Award. (Name) is most deserving of this honor.

Sincerely,

Principal

Recommendation Letter 10.8
PROFESSIONAL AWARD

Elementary or Secondary

(Date)

(Name)

(Address)

Dear (Name):

I recommend (Name) for the (Name of Award) Award presented by (Presenters).

I have known (Name) for the past (Number) years. During that time, (Name) has held the positions of (Position) and of (Position). (Name)'s responsibilities included (Responsibility) and (Responsibility).

(Name) is a strong leader who has unique abilities to mobilize staff, students, parents, and the community to work together to achieve the school's goals. Under the leadership of (Name), the school has accomplished the following:

(Accomplishments)

(Name) is an outstanding (Position) who is an excellent candidate for the (Name of Award) Award. If I can supply any further information in support of (Name)'s nomination, please let me know.

Sincerely,

Principal

Recommendation Letter 10.9
STUDENT JOB APPLICATION

Secondary

(Date)

(Name)

(Address)

Dear (Name):

I am pleased to recommend (Name) as an excellent candidate for the (Position). (Name) has been a student at our school for the past (Number) years, during which time I have known (Him/Her) personally.

(Name) has many characteristics that make (Him/Her) an outstanding candidate for the (Position). (Name) is intelligent and dependable. (He/She) gets along well with others and is exceptionally hardworking. (Name) will be very successful at (Position).

Sincerely,

Principal

Recommendation Letter 10.10
STUDENT ADMISSION

Secondary

(Date)

(Name)

(Address)

Dear (Name):

It is my pleasure to recommend (Name) for admission to (Name of University) University. (Name) is an outstanding student. (His/Her) academic record is excellent. (Name)'s achievements are noteworthy.

(Name) was a member of (Organization #1) for (Number) years, (Organization #2) for (Number) years, and (Organization #3) for (Number) years.

I recommend (Name) without reservation. If I can provide further information, please let me know.

Sincerely,

Principal

11

Job Application Letter

Occasionally, a principal may apply for a new position. A cover letter accompanied by a resume and a list of potential references are typically sent as an application. Following is an example of a letter used in an application for a position.

JOB APPLICATION LETTER 11.1

Elementary or Secondary

(Date)

(Name)

(Address)

Dear (Name):

I would like to be given consideration for the (Position) position announced in the (Journal/Paper). I am currently (Position) at (Name of School) School. I have held this position for (Number) years. Prior to this, I was a (Position) at (Name of School) School for (Number) years. I have had additional experience as a (Position), (Position), and (Position).

I hold a (Name of Degree) degree in (Subject) from (Name of University) University and a (Name of Degree) degree from (Name of University) University. My specialty areas are (Subject) and (Subject). I have had special training in (Subject) and (Subject), which are specific to the requirements stated in the position announcement.

I have included a copy of my resume with this letter. I have also included a list of individuals you might want to contact as references.

If I can provide any further information in support of my application, please call me at (Phone Number) (days) or (Phone Number) (evenings). Thank you for your consideration of this application. I look forward to hearing from you.

Sincerely,

12

Special-Event Invitations

School events are announced through letters and invitations. Special events are important opportunities for building strong parent and community relationships. Invitations should be positive and encouraging because good attendance is a goal. The invitations should provide the important details about the event and sufficient description of the activity to elicit participation.

Invitations to *parents or guardians* might include the following:

Open Houses

Parent-teacher conferences

Special weeks at school

Parent workshops

Special meetings

Fundraising meetings and activities.

Special Event Invitation 12.1
OPEN HOUSE (1)

Elementary or Secondary

(Date)

(Name)

(Address)

Dear (Name):

Open House for families and students will be held (Day of the Week), (Date), at (Time). We hope you will be able to attend. You will be able to visit classes, see demonstrations, and tour the school. We will start with a brief informational presentation at (Time) in (Room at School).

Students will be available to answer questions. Refreshments will be served in the school cafeteria at (Time).

We look forward to seeing you soon.

Sincerely,

Principal

Special Event Invitation 12.2
OPEN HOUSE (2)

Elementary or Secondary

(Date)

(Name)

(Address)

Dear (Name):

The (Name of School) School Open House will be held on (Day of the Week), (Date), from (Time) to (Time). You are also invited to meet with the Parent-Teacher Association from (Time) to (Time) in the (Room of School).

We look forward to seeing you on (Date).

Sincerely,

Principal

Special Event Invitation 12.3
PARENT-TEACHER CONFERENCE (1)

Secondary

(Date)

Dear Parents:

Parent-teacher conferences for second semester will be from (Time) to (Time), (Date) and (Date). Each teacher is limited to conferences of no longer than seven minutes. It may not be possible for teachers to have conferences with every parent in the time allotted.

A schedule and an appointment form have been provided to help you identify the teachers you want to see. Please ask your son or daughter to fill in the schedule form with the subjects he or she is taking and the names of the teachers.

Time labels for each teacher will be posted in the (Room Number) by (Time) on the day of the conferences (one hour before the first scheduled conference time). To arrange for a teacher conference, remove one label for each teacher you wish to see and place it on your appointment form.

If all of the time labels for a specific teacher have been taken, that teacher will not be able to see you on conference night. You will need to call (School Office) to set up a different conference time to meet with that teacher.

School staff will be available to help arrange your conferences. Please do not hesitate to ask for help.

Sincerely,

Principal

Special Event Invitation 12.4
PARENT-TEACHER CONFERENCE (2)

Elementary or Secondary

(Date)

(Name)

(Address)

Dear (Name):

Parent-teacher conferences will be held on (Day of Week), (Date) from (Time) p.m. to (Time) p.m. and on (Day of the Week), (Date) from (Time) a.m. to (Time) a.m. in the (Room at School). The conferences provide an opportunity to meet with teachers to discuss student progress. Conference times with individual teachers will be approximately 15 minutes long to allow teachers to visit with as many people as possible.

This is an excellent opportunity for you to visit with teachers about your child's progress during the first grading period. If you cannot attend a conference on these dates, please call (Phone Number) to arrange an alternate time.

We look forward to your participation.

Sincerely,

Principal

Special Event Invitation 12.5
SPECIAL WEEK

Elementary

(Date)

(Name)

(Address)

Dear (Name):

On (Day of the Week), (Date), and (Day of the Week) at (Time), we will be celebrating (Name of Week) Week.

On (Date), we are asking all parents to join us for (Meal) at (Time) and on (Date), to join us for (Event). We would love to have you come and join us at (Time). After both events, we are going to read books to students, and the students would love to have you read to them or share the story time.

If you are able to come on either of these two dates and then stay to read, please call (Phone Number).

We hope to see you soon.

Sincerely,

Principal

Special Event Invitation 12.6
WORKSHOP

Elementary

(Date)

(Name)

(Address)

Dear (Name):

You are invited to a special Parent Workshop on (Day of the Week), (Date), from (Time) to (Time). The speaker will be (Name) and the topic will be (Subject). The workshop will introduce activities you can use at home with your child as well as information about your child's needs at this age. You will also have the opportunity to visit with other parents.

Refreshments will be served.

We hope you will be able to attend this special workshop.

Sincerely,

Principal

Special Event Invitation 12.7
PLANNING MEETING

Elementary or Secondary

(Date)

(Name)

(Address)

Dear (Name):

You are invited to attend our school district's strategic planning session on (Subject) on (Date) from (Time) to (Time) in the (Name of School) school auditorium. The session leader will be (Name).

The session will begin with a presentation to the whole group followed by small group meetings.

We hope you will be able to participate in this important meeting. If you have any questions, please call me at (Phone Number).

Sincerely,

Principal

Special Event Invitation 12.8
MEETING

Elementary or Secondary

(Date)

(Name)

(Address)

Dear (Name):

The next meeting of the (Name of Council) Council will be at (Time) on (Date) in (Room Number). A tentative agenda for the meeting is enclosed. We expect (Name), (Name), and (Name) to attend.

As you know, the (Name of Council) Council is the (Description) for the school. The purpose of the meeting is to improve achievement and learning opportunities for all students.

We look forward to your participation.

Sincerely,

Principal

Special Event Invitation 12.9
FUNDRAISING PLANNING

Elementary

(Date)

Dear Parents:

The Playground Project has had a successful beginning to its fundraising campaign. Currently, our fundraising efforts have totaled approximately (Dollar Amount).

As the committee considered projects for next year, they decided that more ideas and input are needed. We hope we can count on you for support and participation.

A planning meeting has been scheduled for (Date) in Room (Room Number) at the (Name of School) School. We hope you will be able to attend.

Sincerely,

Principal

Special Event Invitation 12.10
BUSINESS DONATION
FOR FUNDRAISING

Elementary

(Date)

(Name)

(Address)

Dear (Name):

The Parent-Teacher Organization at (Name of School) School has organized a fundraising drive for new playground equipment. We have two activities planned and hope your business will be able to make a donation. On (Date), we will hold a carnival and we would like to have door prizes. We will also hold a raffle of larger items. Raffle ticket sales will begin on (Date) with winners selected on (Date) at (Event).

Please consider donating an item that could be used as either a raffle item or a door prize. We will call you next week to discuss a possible donation. All donations will be collected by (Date).

Thank you for considering this request. If you have any questions, please call me at (Phone Number).

Sincerely,

Principal

Special Event Invitation 12.11
FUNDRAISING PARTICIPATION
FOR PARENTS (1)

Elementary

HOLIDAY GREETINGS

During past years, the parent group at (Name of School) has been responsible for making many special purchases for the (Description). These are usually things that are not included in the (Type of Budget) budget.

Without parent support of fundraisers, children would not have many of the special things that make their school day a fun learning experience.

Work is already in progress for the (Name of Fundraiser). This is our largest fundraiser for the year, and we need your help. When you see a request for volunteers, please sign up. This is a great way to get to know other families and show your child that good things happen when we all work together.

Take a look at the items listed below and see how past contributions have helped make (Name of School) a terrific place for kids.

Thank you and Happy Holidays from the (Name of School)!

Outdoor Items	*Shared Items*	*Miscellaneous Items*
Tricycles	Computers	Field Trips
Playhouse	Musical Instruments	Teacher Appreciation
Sand & Sand Toys	Hardcover Books	Telephones in All Rooms
	Balance Beam	

Special Event Invitation 12.12
FUNDRAISING PARTICIPATION
FOR PARENTS (2)

Elementary

THE IMPORTANCE OF THE (NAME OF SCHOOL) FUND
AND HOW IT SUPPORTS OUR SCHOOL

Each year, the (Name of School) Parent-Teacher Organization (PTO) supports our school with additional funds. The PTO has made the following contributions:

(Contributions)

This year, the PTO will be contributing funds to special events. The PTO also sponsors teacher recognitions and many other special projects throughout the year.

The (Name of School) Fund was started in (Year) as our only source of fundraising (no door-to-door sales). We have estimated that if each family could contribute $25, we would raise approximately $10,000. The fund is clearly the easiest way to raise this amount of money with only two volunteers chairing the event. If you have ever been involved in a fundraiser, you know that it requires a lot of time and volunteers.

Each grade level will be given an equal amount of money. The PTO will be gathering ideas and voting on projects at scheduled PTO meetings. All PTO expenditures are discussed and voted on at the regular PTO meetings.

Any contribution you can make to the Fund will be appreciated!

If you have any questions or suggestions, please contact me.

Sincerely,

Principal

13

Opening Comments
for Special Events

Although not strictly letters, the examples given in this chapter can certainly be time savers for busy principals. As a principal, you have many speaking opportunities. School programs, awards and honors ceremonies, civic activities, parent meetings, and celebrations are some of the events that provide speaking opportunities. As you prepare for these events, consider the following issues:

Who is the audience? (Obviously, we talk differently to children than to adults.)

How will I elicit the interest of the audience?

How will I make my presentation memorable for the audience?

What are the main ideas I want to convey to the audience?

How much time is available for the presentation?

Examples of opening comments you may be asked to provide can include the following:

Open Houses

Awards ceremonies

Special ceremonies

Conferences

Nominating candidates for offices

Opening Comments 13.1
OPEN HOUSE

Elementary

Welcome to the (Name of School) Open House. I am (Name), principal of (Name of School). I am pleased that you are here tonight. We have a long tradition of providing a fine educational setting for teaching and learning.

As you know, our school mission is (Mission).

We must work together to achieve that mission. We know that today's children will face challenges and opportunities we cannot even imagine this afternoon. As partners in their education, we must prepare them for their exciting future.

Our schedule for this evening is (Schedule).

Thank you for coming to the Open House. Your support and interest are essential to the children's positive school experiences.

Opening Comments 13.2
AWARD CEREMONY (1)

Elementary or Secondary

Good Evening! This is a great opportunity to recognize the accomplishments of our students.

The (Name of Award) is presented to an outstanding individual who (Criteria for Award).

Tonight we recognize this individual's accomplishment (State the individual's accomplishment).

A committee of judges consisting of (Names and Positions) determined the winner of this award.

The criteria used in the selection were (Criteria).

The winner is (Name).

Present the award and shake hands with the winner. Ask the person to make a few remarks.

Opening Comments 13.3
AWARD CEREMONY (2)

Elementary or Secondary

Good Evening. (Name of Award) Award is presented to an outstanding individual who has provided exceptional service to education. Tonight, we are here to recognize the accomplishments of an outstanding individual and present the (Name of Award) Award.

The selection committee for this award consisted of representatives from the state department of education, the school board, the city parks and recreation department, and the YMCA. The pool of candidates was outstanding. Selecting a winner was clearly a challenge.

To be a candidate for this award, the person must be an active member of educational organizations, must have been involved in education for five or more years, and must be currently active in a specific education project.

The winner of the (Name of Award) Award is (Name). Among (Name)'s activities are the following: (List activities)

It is a pleasure to present this Award to (Name).

Opening Comments 13.4
SPECIAL CEREMONY

Elementary or Secondary

Thank you for coming to this special ceremony to dedicate and name our new (Building/Center) in honor of (Name). (Name) was the (Position) from (Year) to (Year). During (Name)'s tenure in this position, (He/She) accomplished the following (Accomplishment), (Accomplishment), (Accomplishment), and (Accomplishment). The naming of the (Building/Center) in honor of (Name) is especially appropriate because (Name) had a special interest in (Name of School). This reflects (Name)'s commitment to this aspect of education. Many of you have contributed in special ways to make (Building/Center) possible. Thank you again for your efforts. It's great to see what we are able to accomplish when we set goals for ourselves.

We are particularly pleased that (Name) is here today, accompanied by (His/Her) family members. We are pleased to be able to enjoy this special event with them. We hope (Name) will share a few comments with us, too.

Opening Comments 13.5
INTRODUCING CONFERENCE SPEAKER

Elementary or Secondary

Good afternoon. It is a pleasure to introduce our conference speaker, the Director of (Department). As we begin this new era, (Name)'s topic, (Name of Topic), is especially timely.

This is how the demographics of our country have changed: (Comparative Demographics of the United States).

This is how the demographics of our community have changed: (Comparative Demographics of the Community).

Today, our keynote speaker, (Name), will share (Description). In addition to (Name)'s important role with (Organization), (Name) is the (Description). (Name) earned (His/Her) bachelor's degree in (Department/Specialty) from the University of (Name of University), and (He/She) earned a master's degree from (Name of University) in (Department/Specialty). We are fortunate to have (Name) as our speaker today, and I am pleased to present (Name) to you.

Opening Comments 13.6
CONFERENCE

Elementary or Secondary

Good afternoon! Welcome to the (Number) Annual (Name of Conference) Conference sponsored by the (Name of Sponsor). During the past (Number) years, this conference has addressed the issue of (Subject of Conference). Our efforts have resulted in (Accomplishments). For these reasons, I am proud to be a member of the organization, and it gives me great pleasure to welcome you here.

Today, more than (Number) are in attendance at this conference where we will address the critical issue of (Subject). As we begin a new era, we want to (Goals for the Future).

Again, welcome to the (Number) Annual (Name of Conference) Conference. We hope it will be an outstanding experience for you.

Opening Comments 13.7
NOMINATION

Elementary or Secondary

I am pleased to nominate (Name) for the office of (Position) of the (Name of Organization). This position requires a dedicated individual who can (Qualifications). The person must be able to work effectively with the members, including (Qualification), (Qualification), and (Qualification). (Name) has served as (Position) for (Number) years. (Name) has also been an active contributor to (Organization), (Organization), and (Organization). (Name) has a commitment to this organization as evidenced by (His/Her) work as (Position), (Position), and (Position) during the past (Number) years.

Because of (Name)'s qualifications, I am confident that coupled with (His/Her) experiences and fine people skills, (Name) will be excellent in the position of (Position).

Thank you for the opportunity to present this nomination.

CORWIN
PRESS